Mother's Day

Coloring Book

Adult Colouring Books

Aryla Publishing 2018

978 1 912675 00 5

www.arylapublishing.com

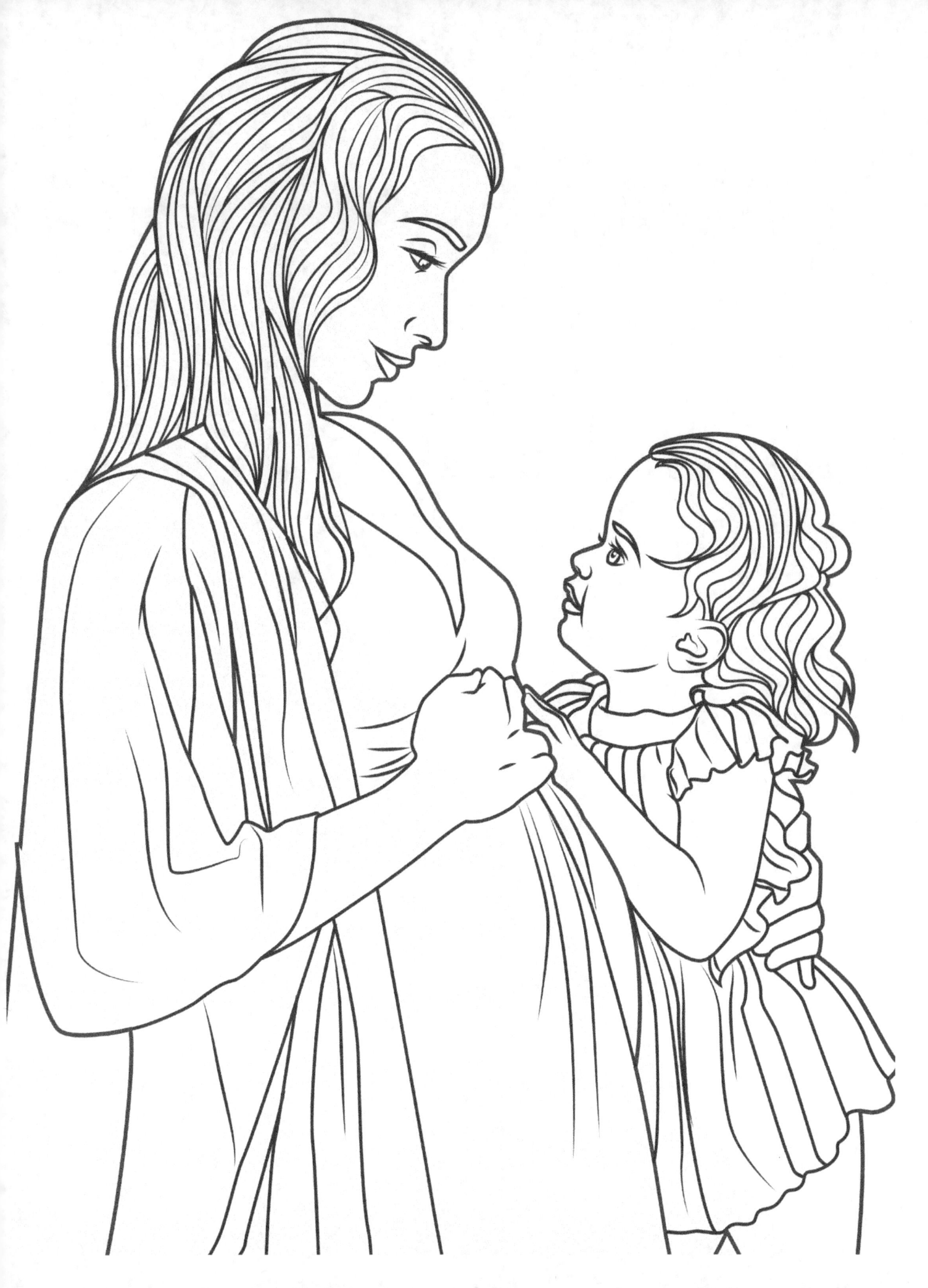

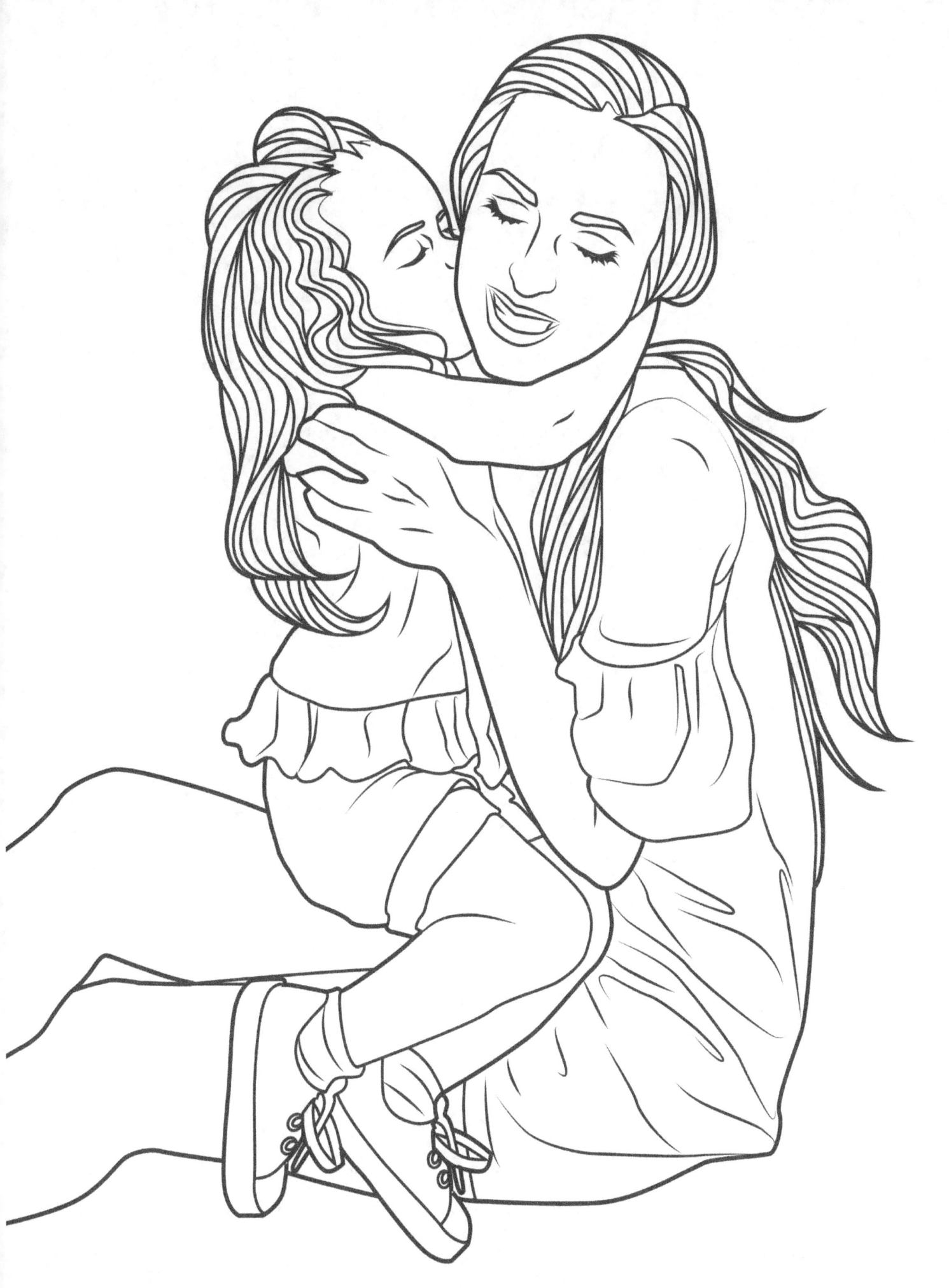

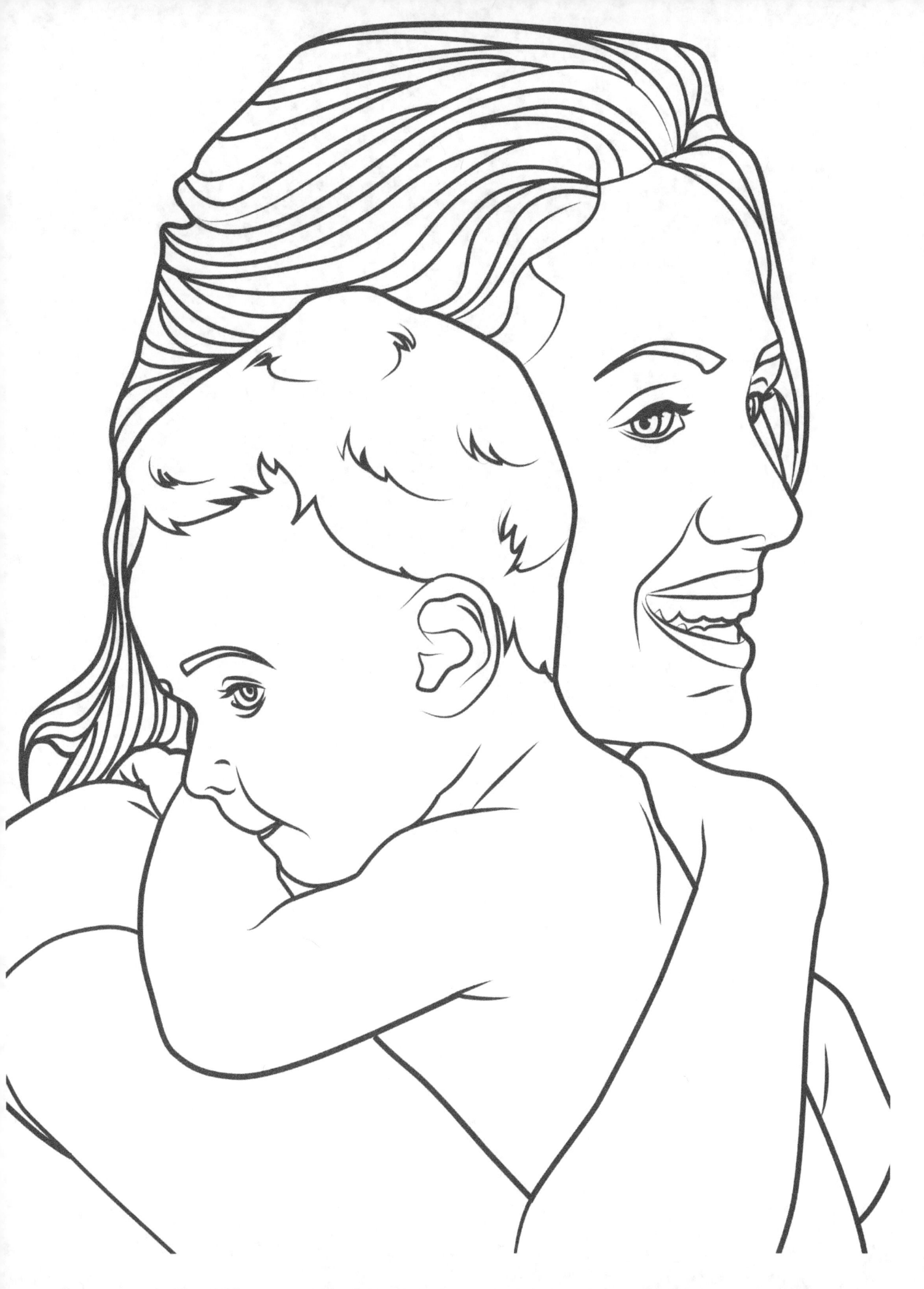

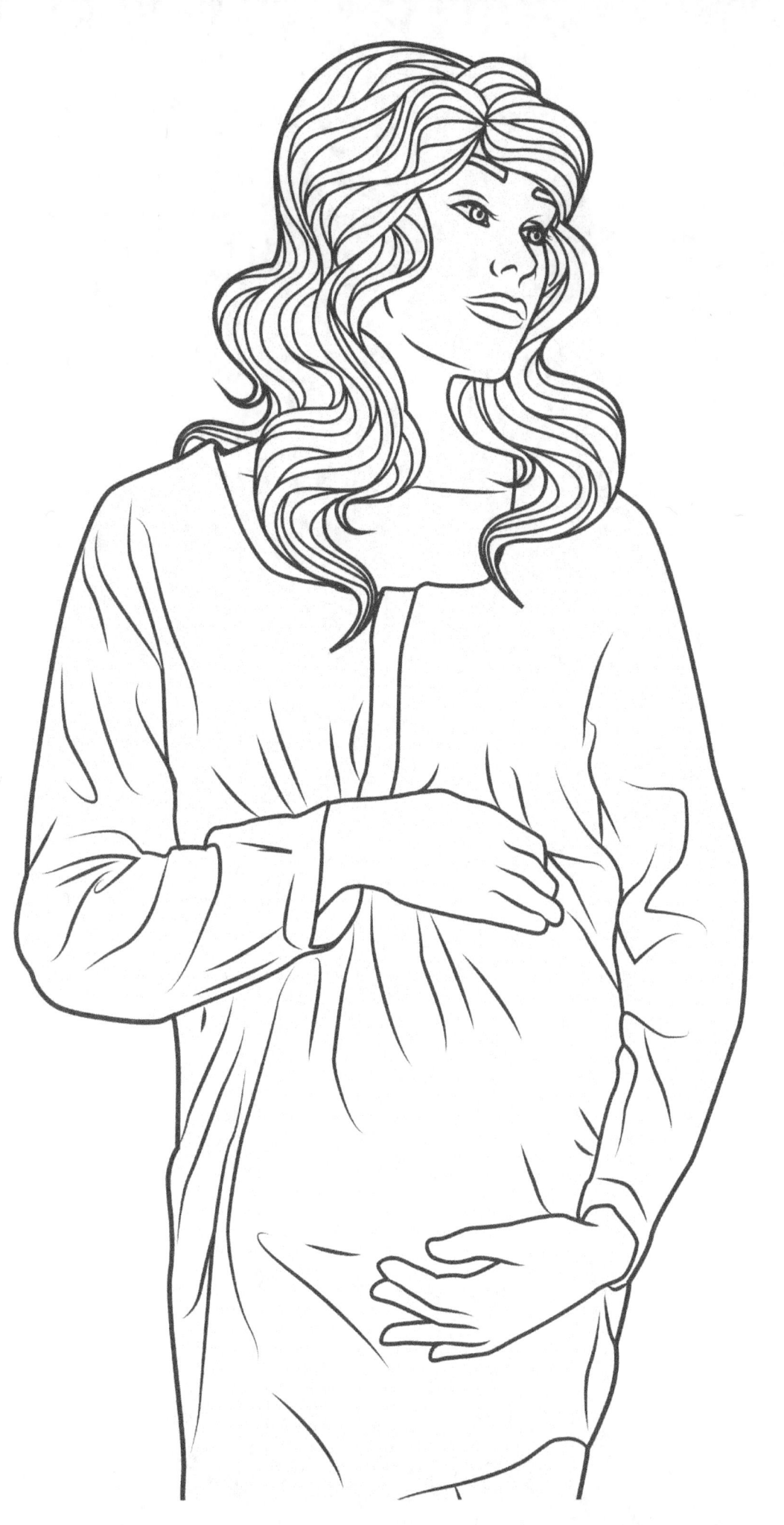

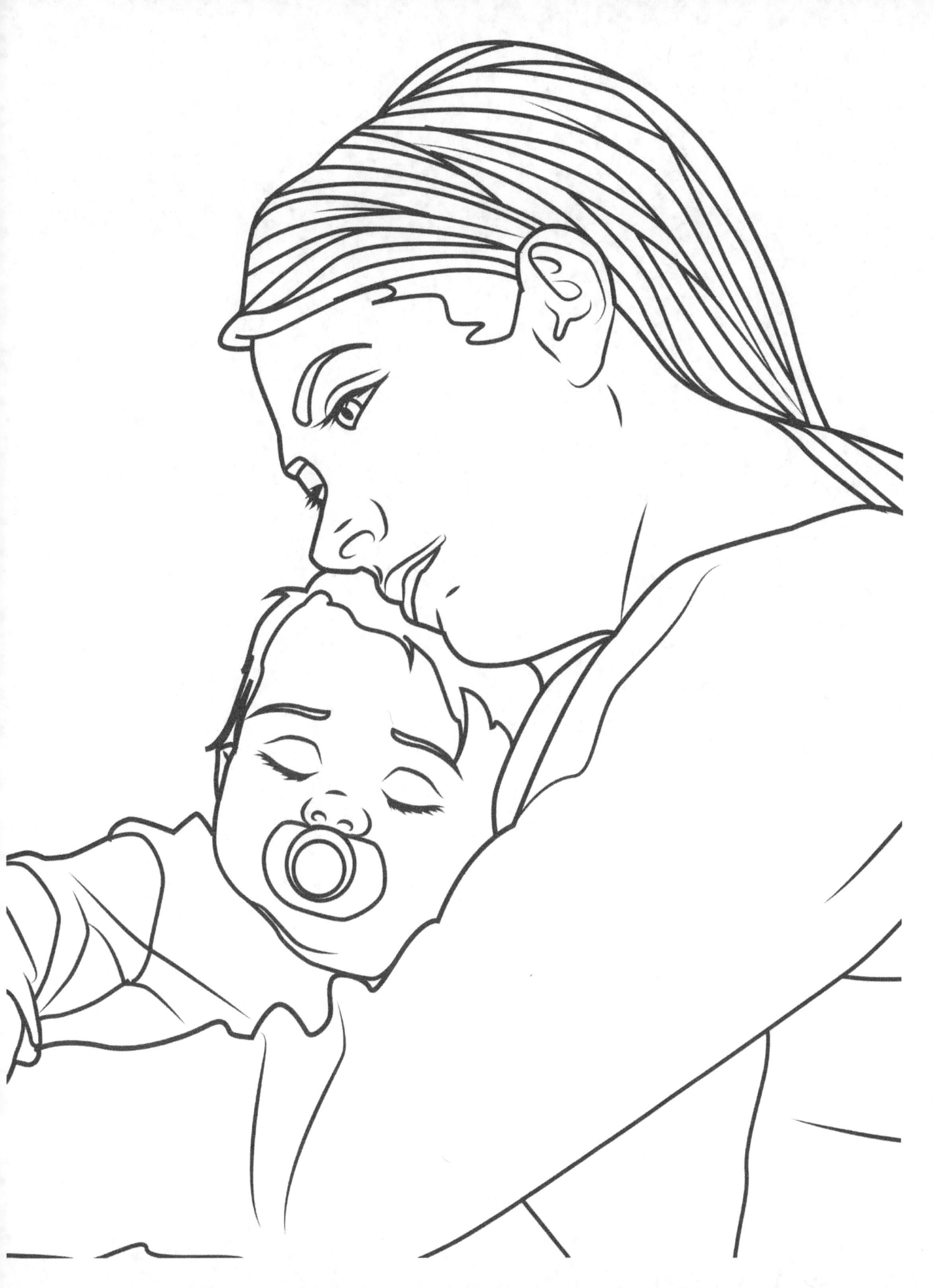

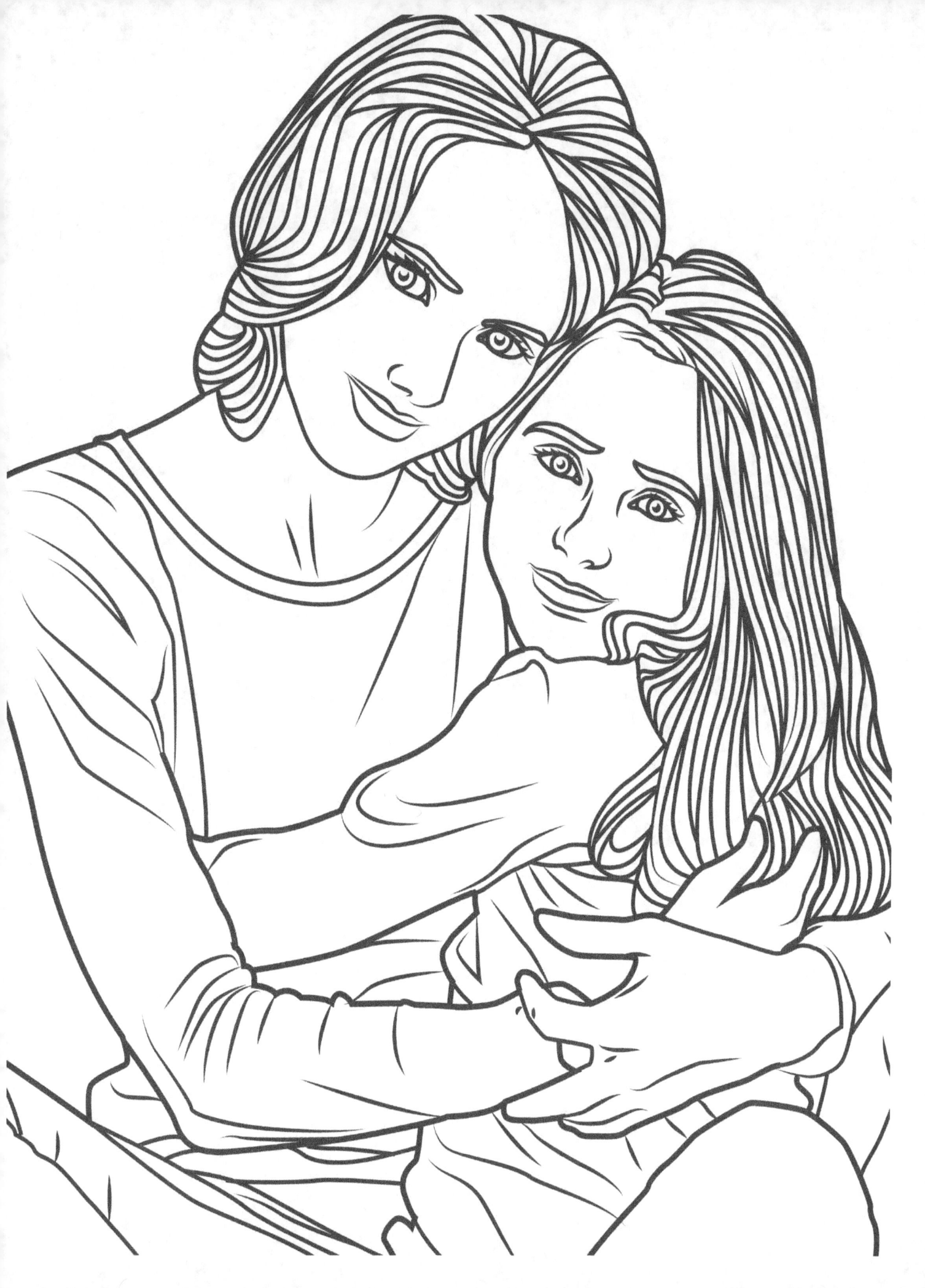

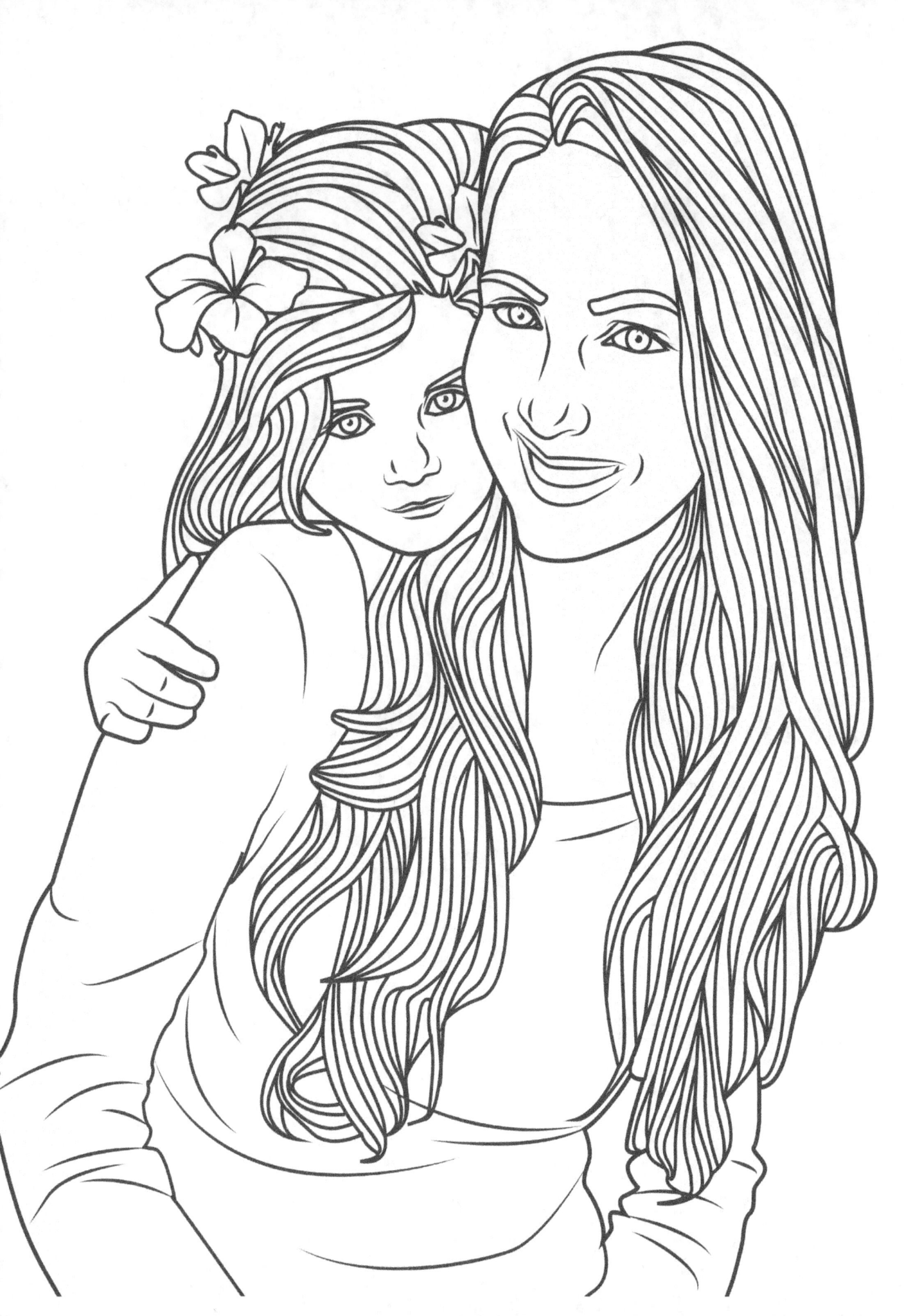

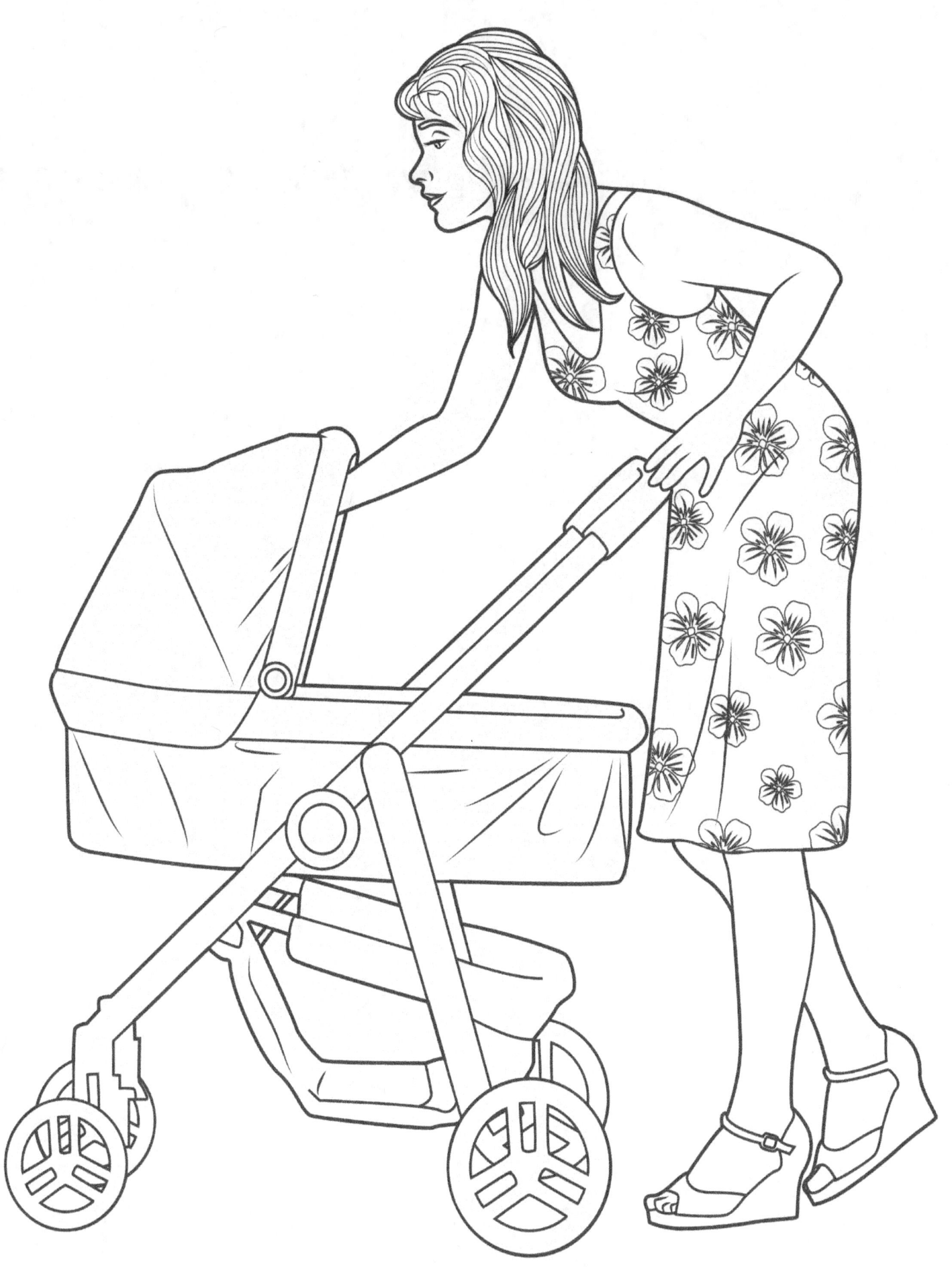

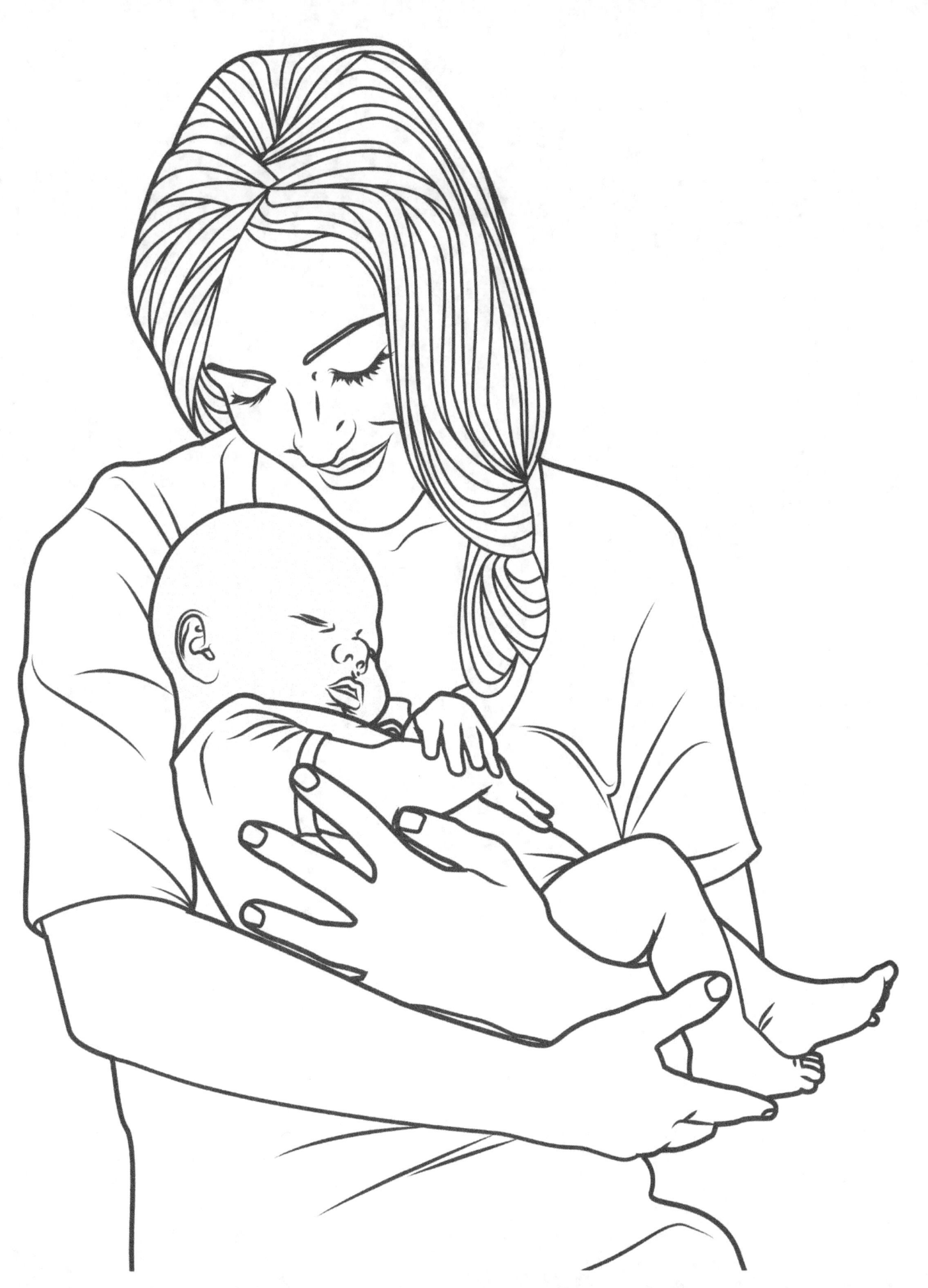

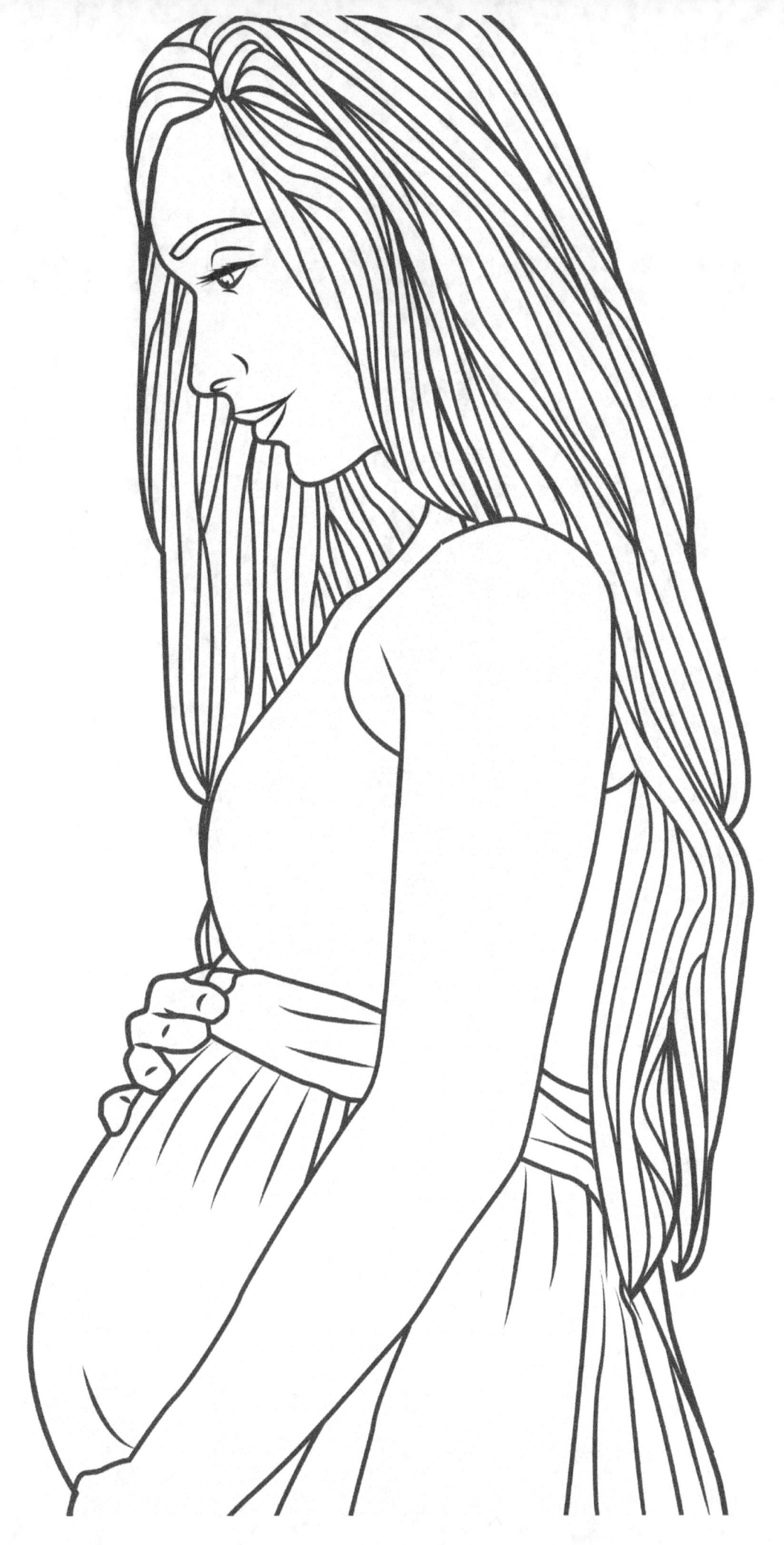

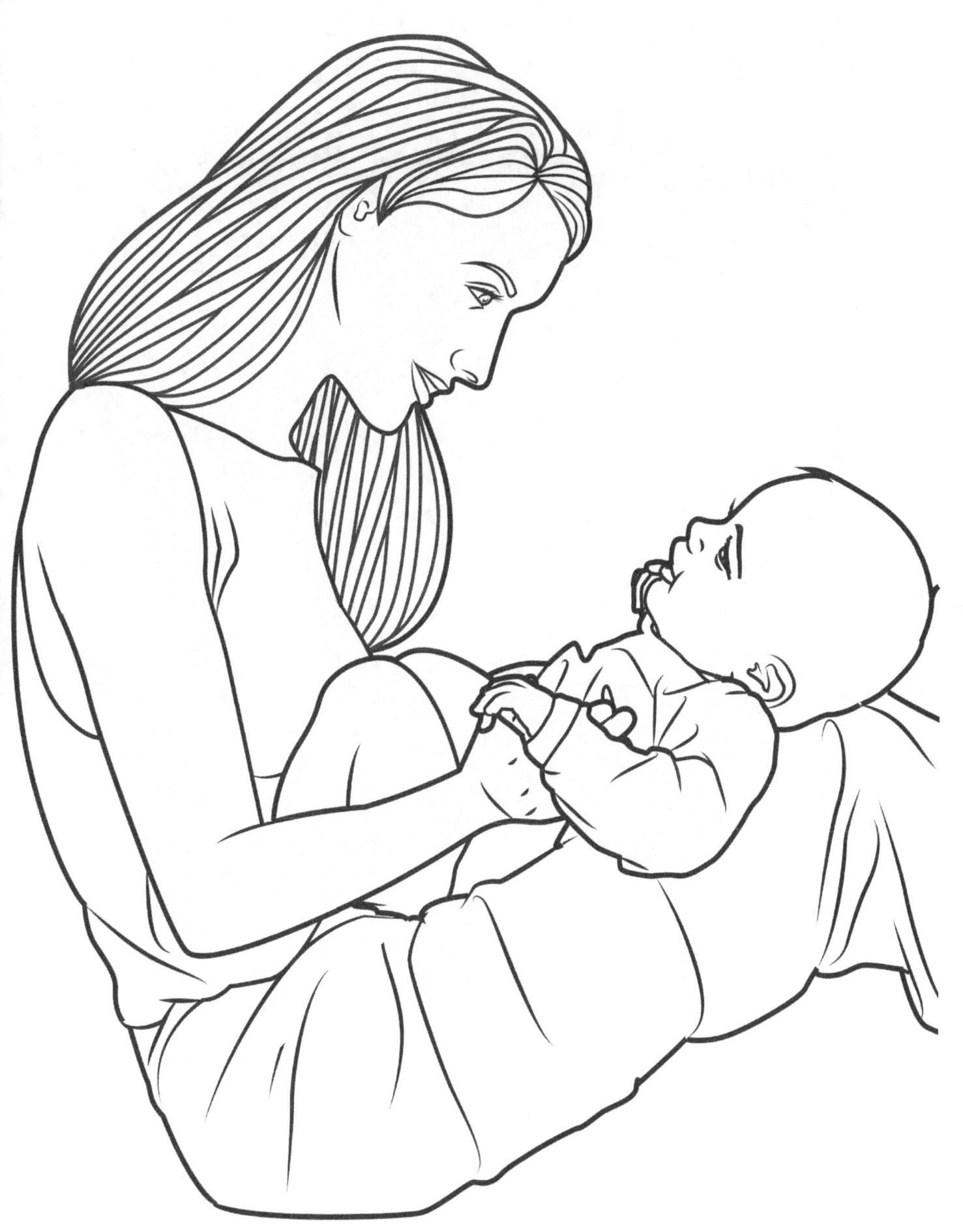

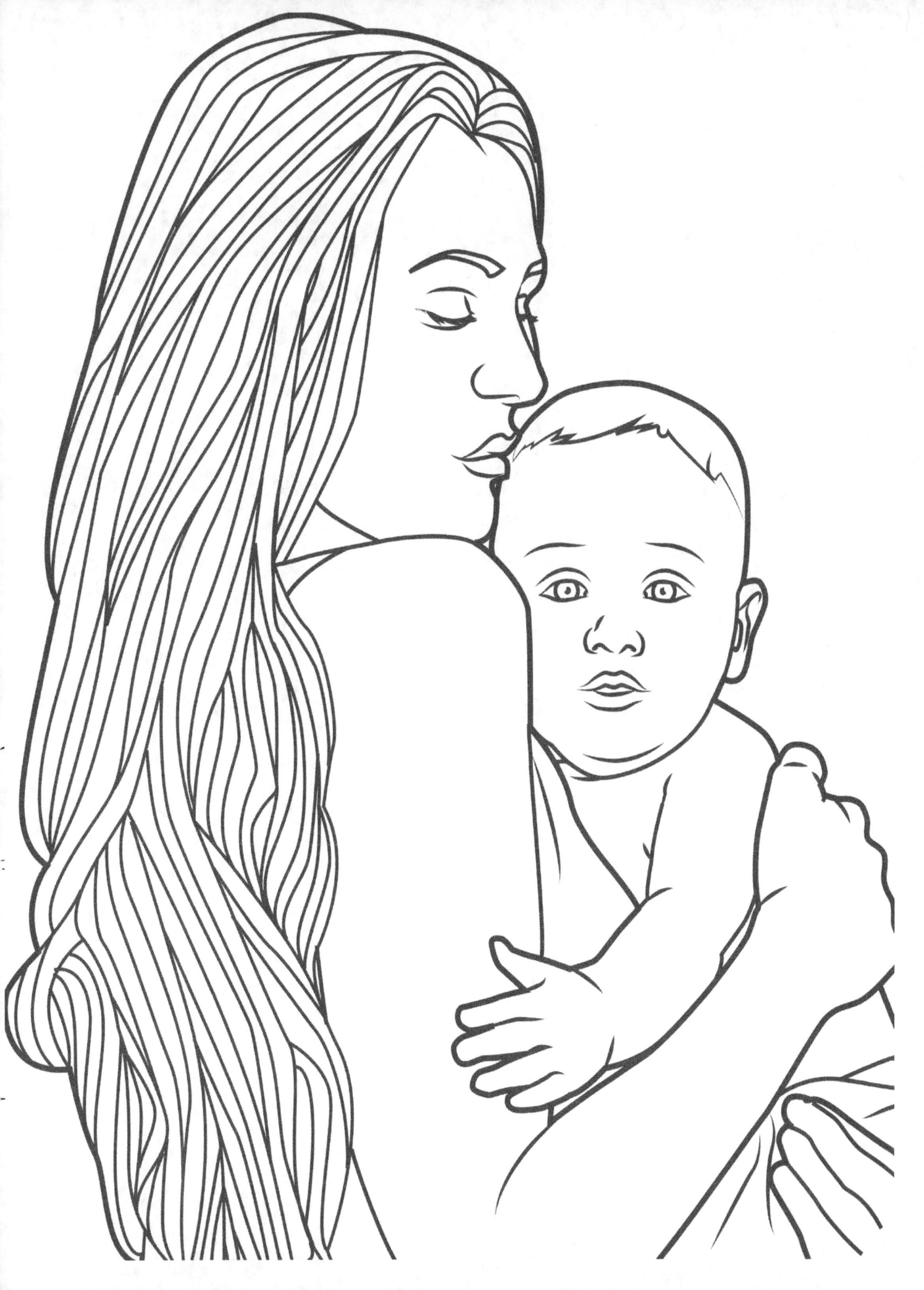

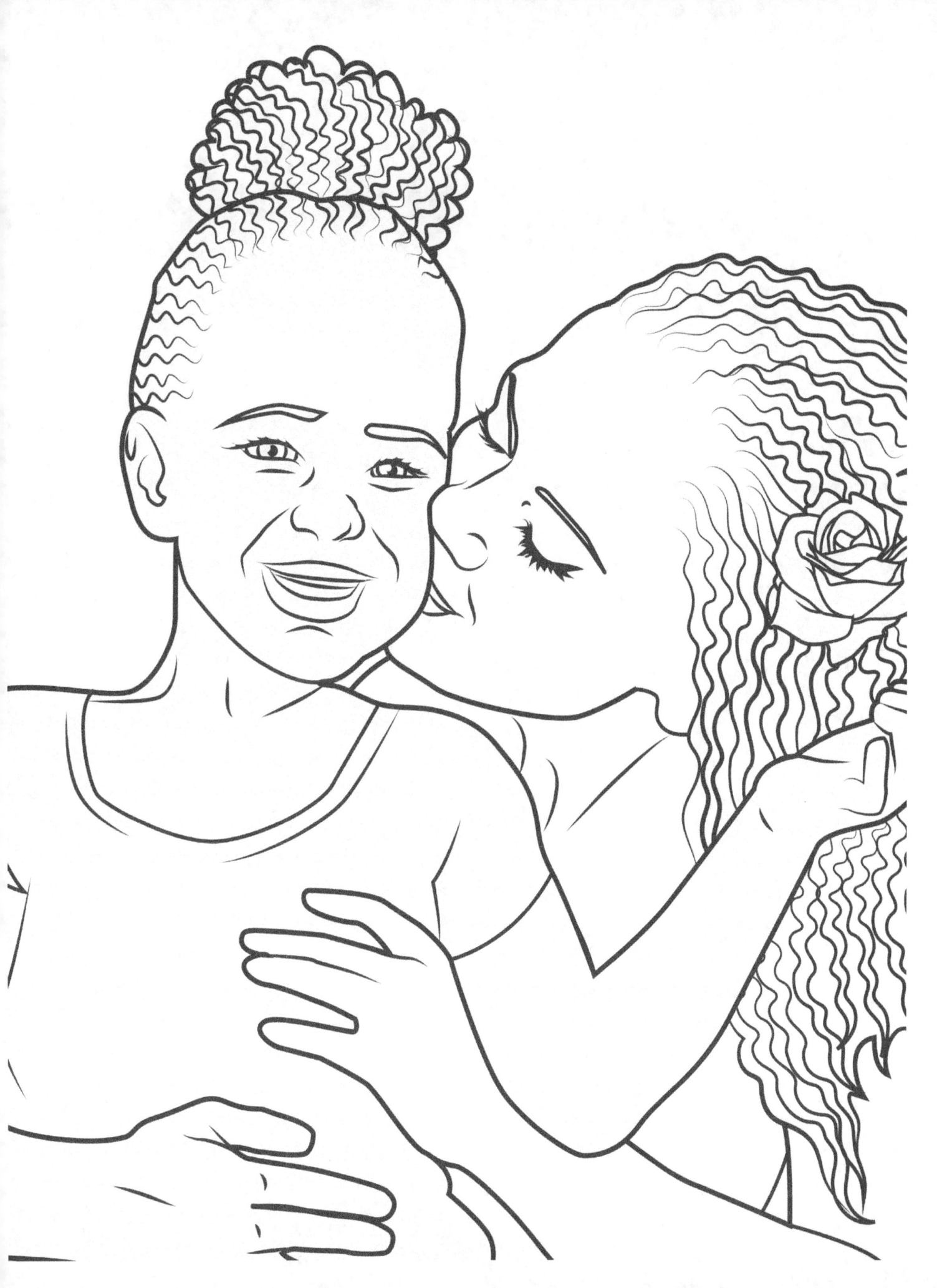

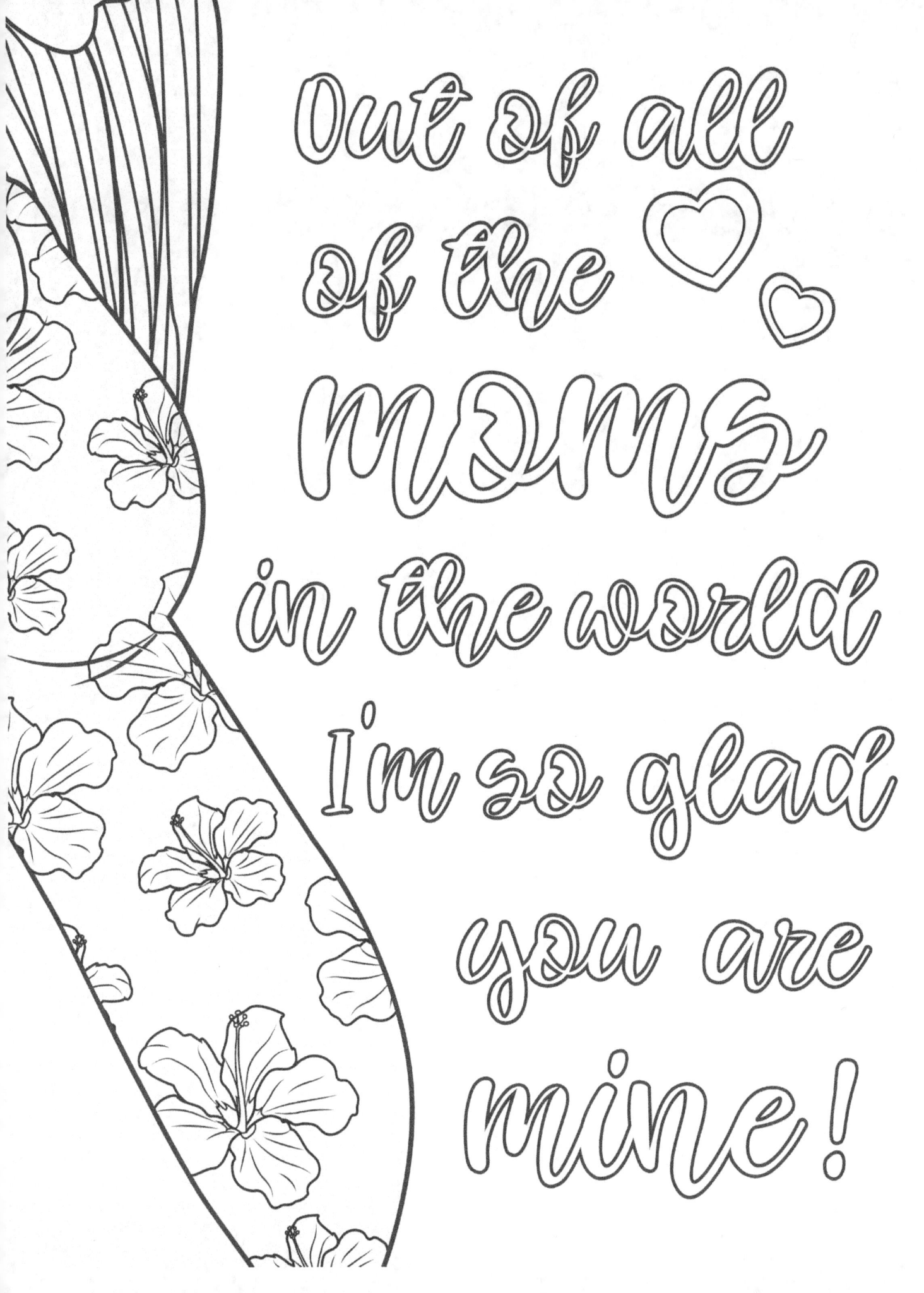

Out of all
of the ♡
moms
in the world
I'm so glad
you are
mine!

best mom ever

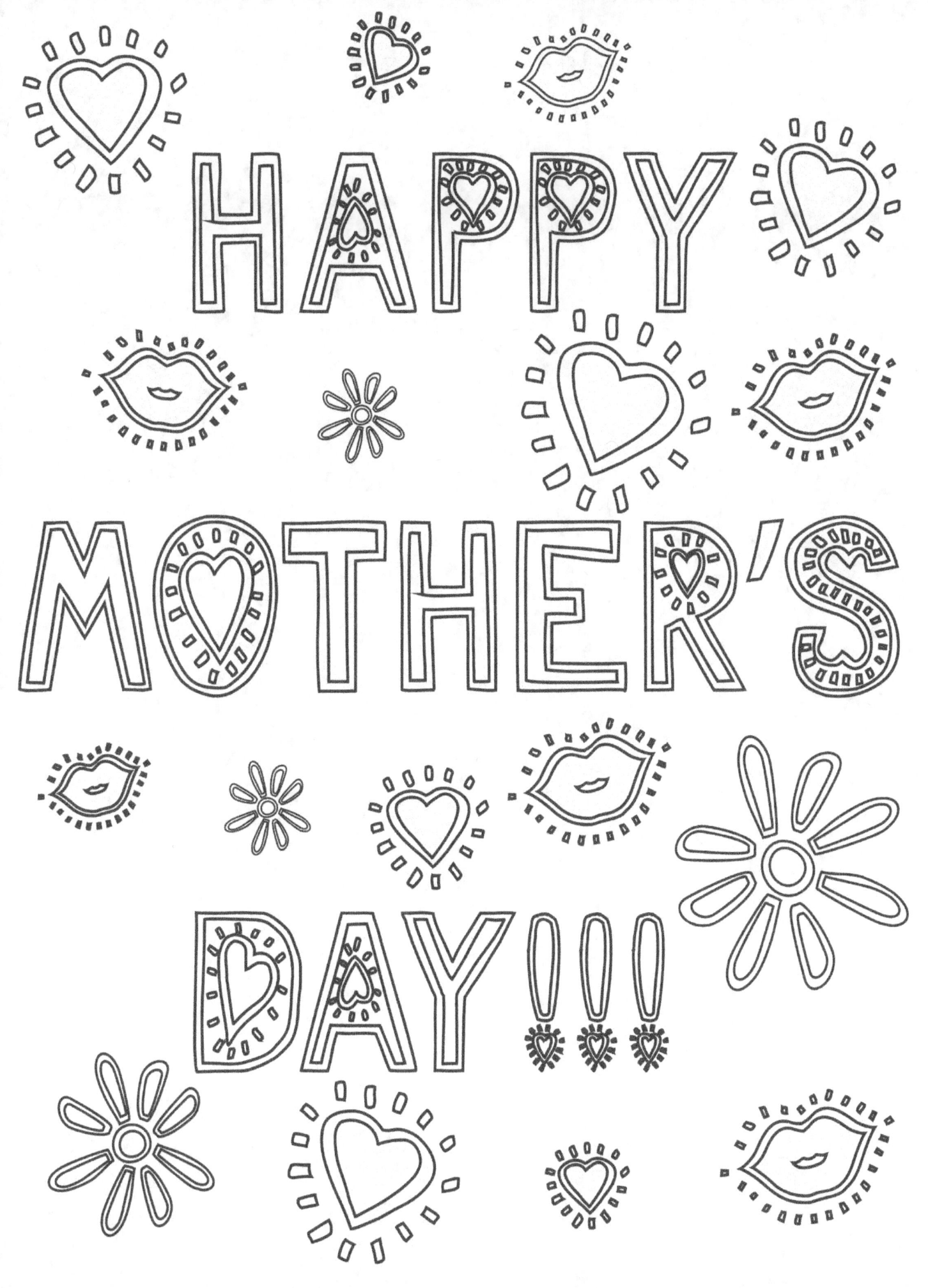

HOME IS WHEREVER MOM IS

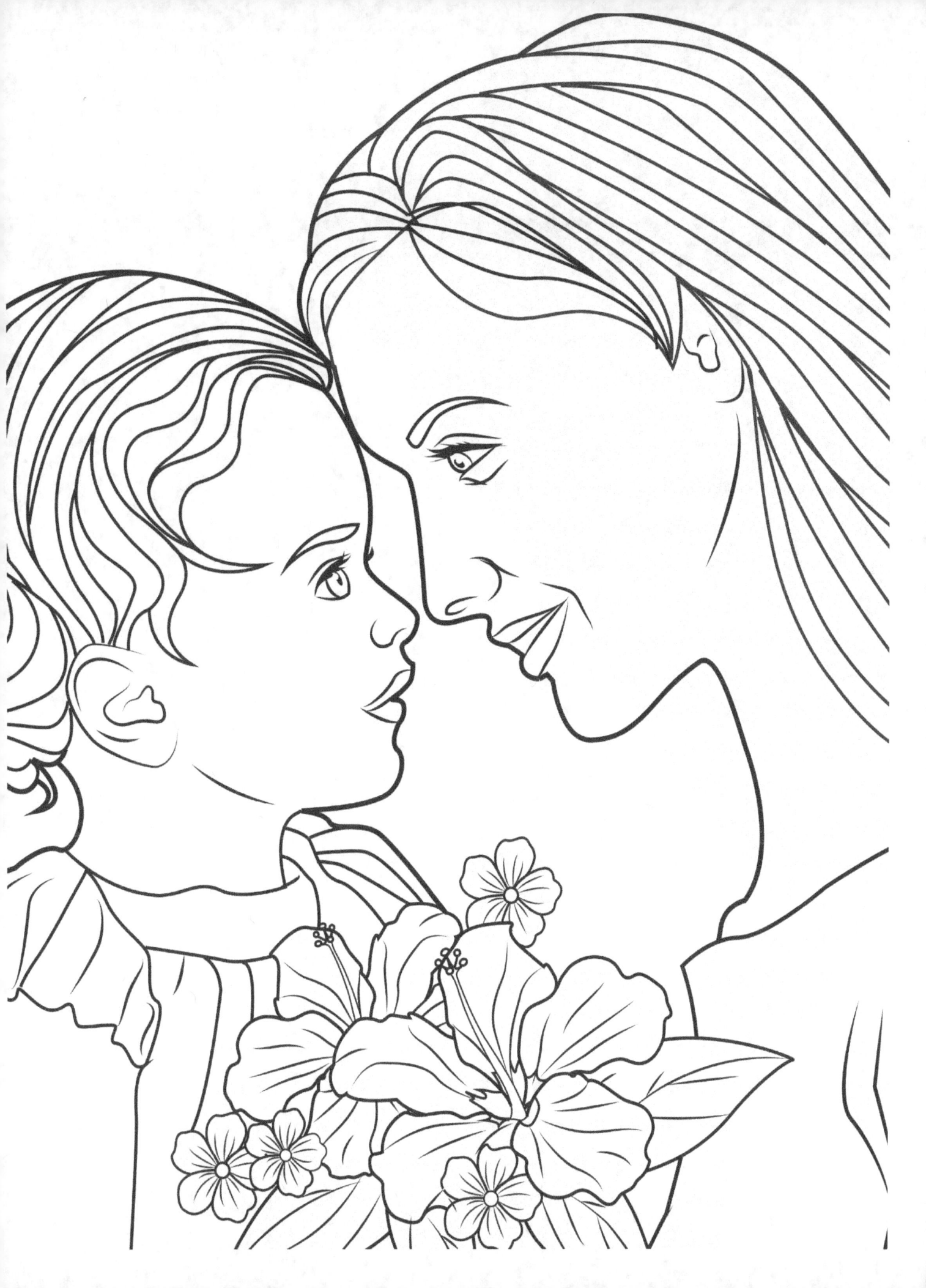

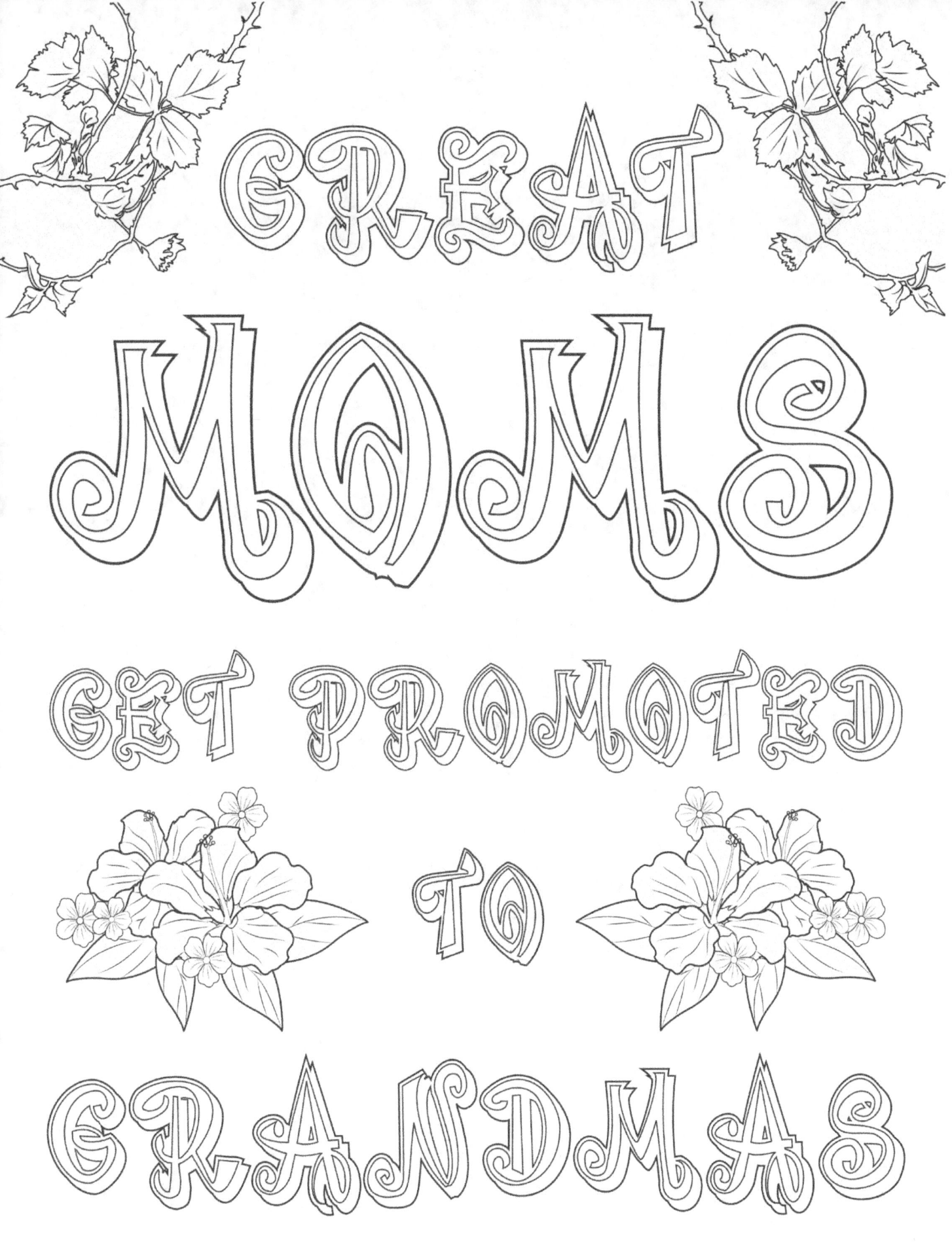

mothers

hold their

children's hands

for a while,

but their hearts

forever.

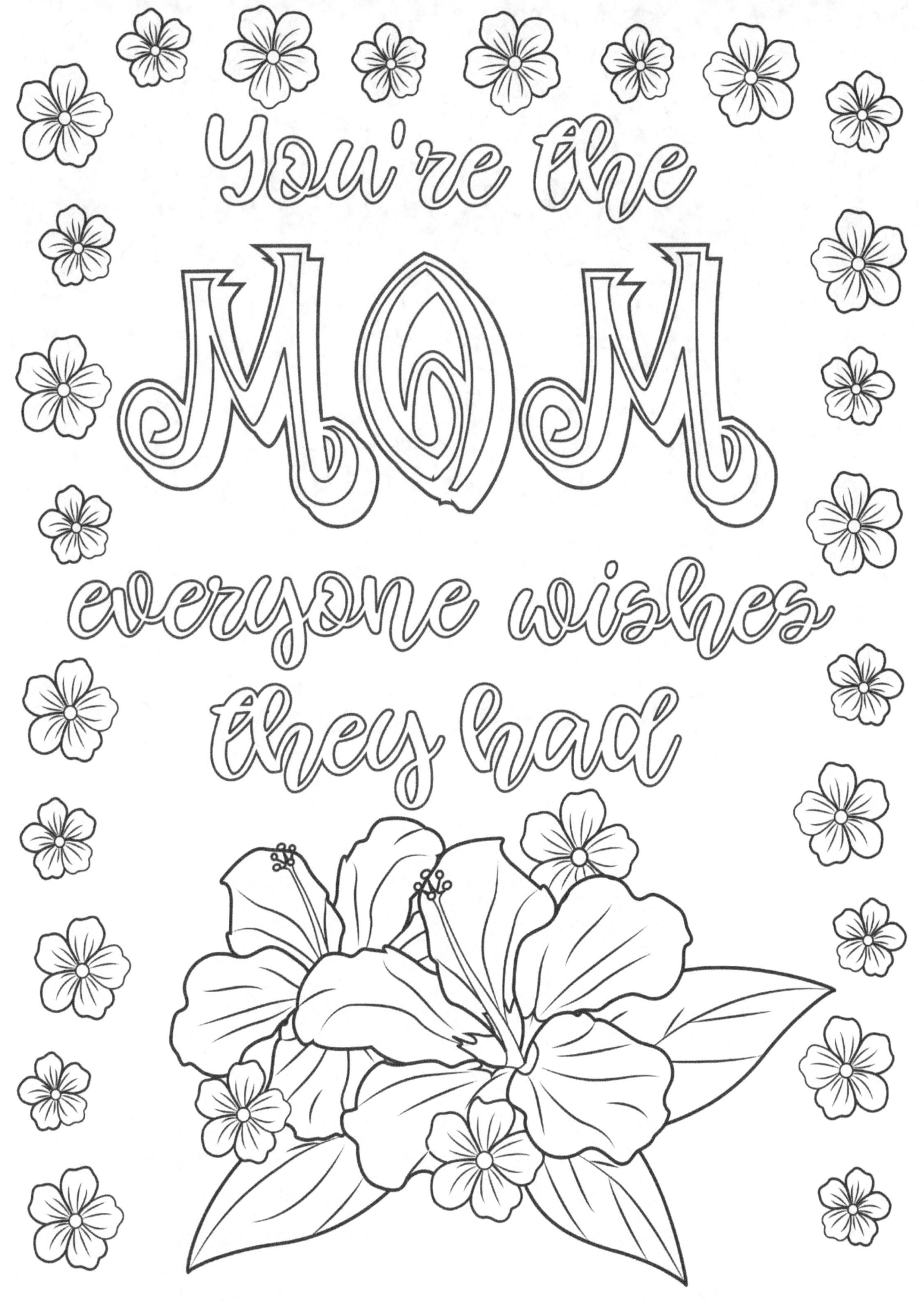

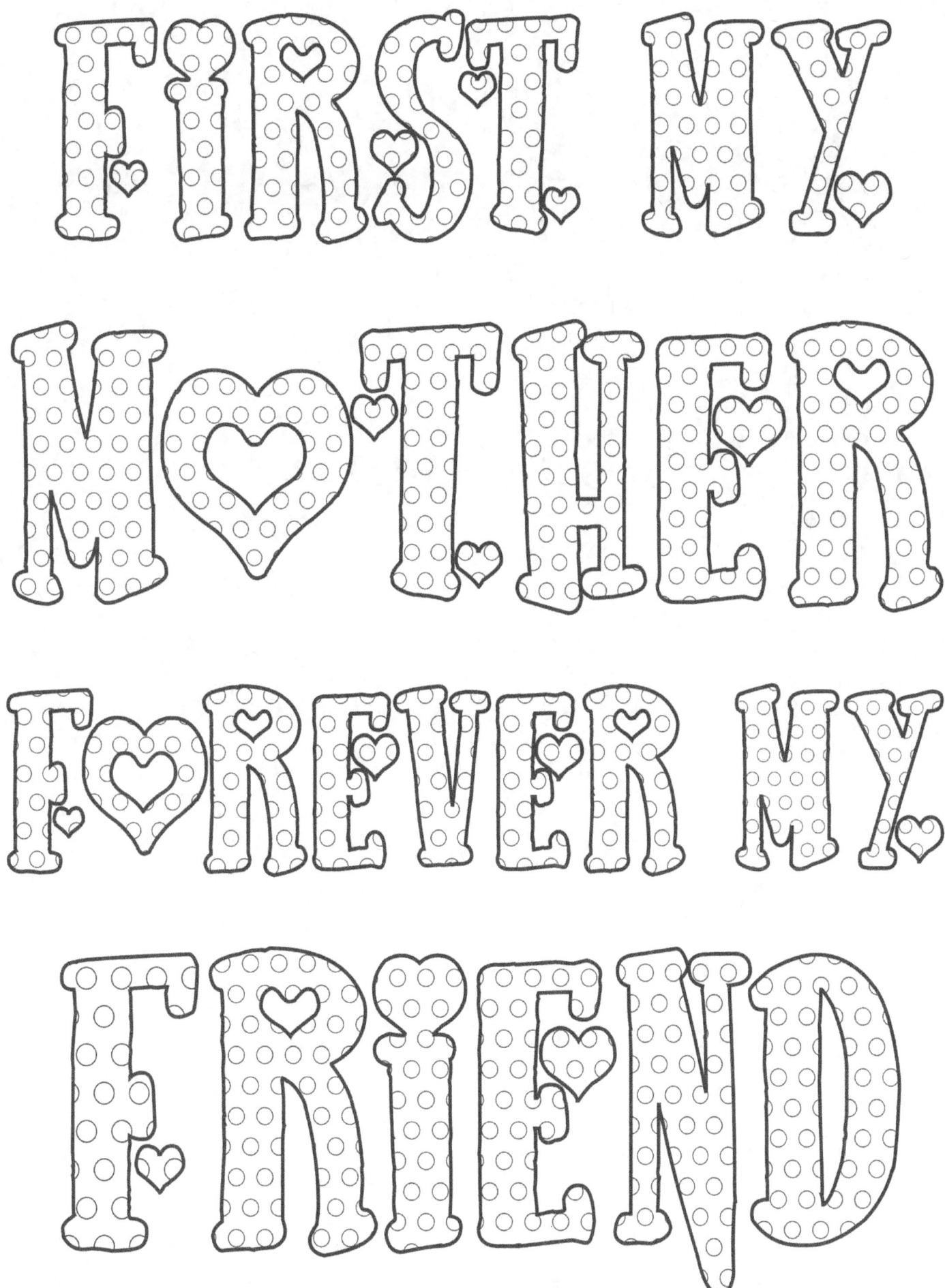

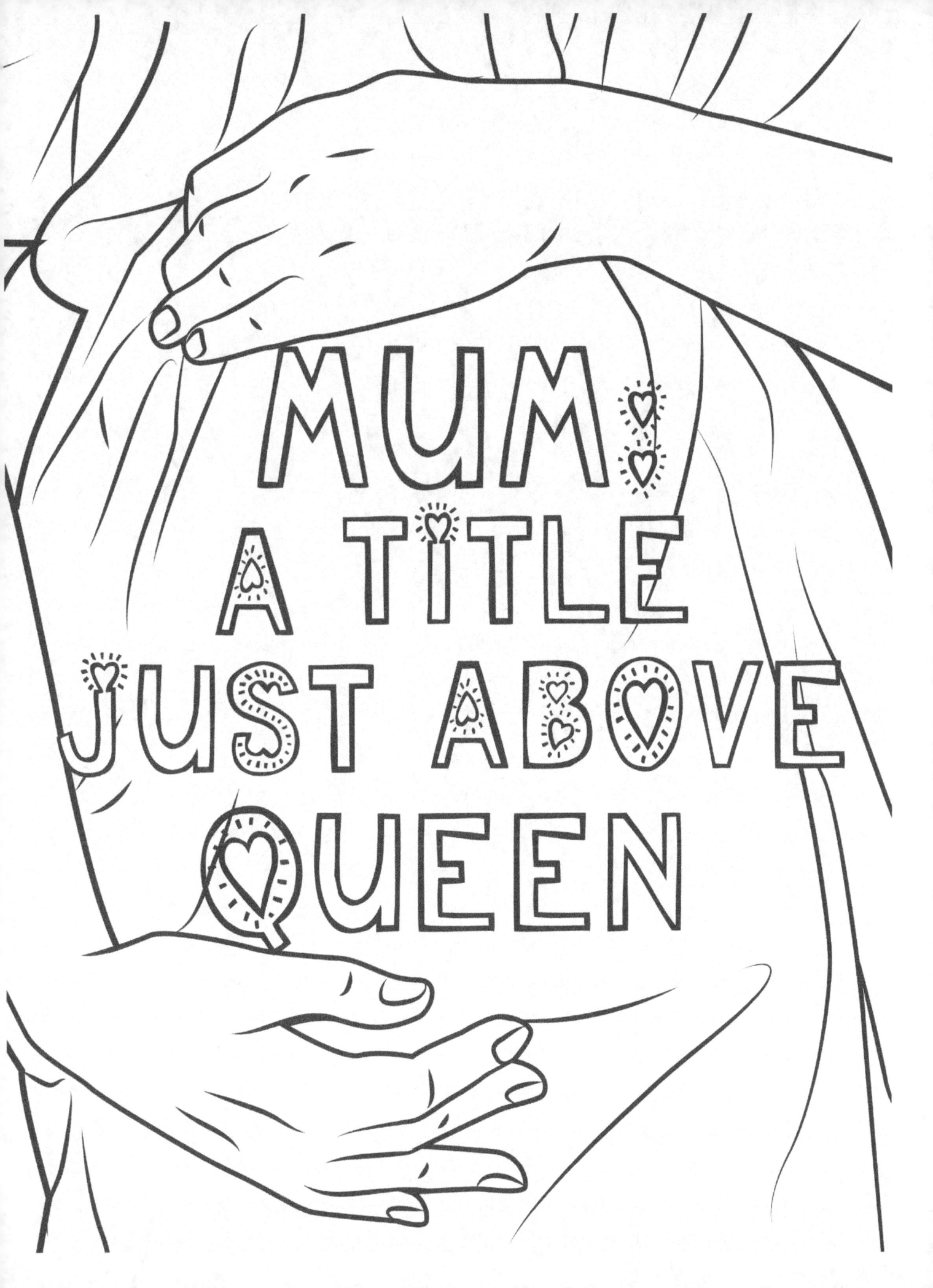

AIN'T NO HOOD LIKE MOTHERHOOD

Thank you for purchasing this book.

If you would like to know more about Aryla Publishing Books please visit:-

www.ArylaPublishing.com

Or follow us on
Facebook
Twitter
Instagram
for *free promotions*

@arylapublishing

We would love to know what you think of this book so please leave us a review.

Have a wonderful day ☺

Other Coloring Books from Aryla Publishing

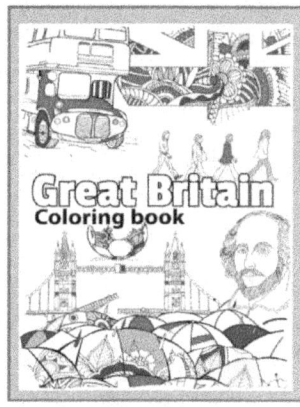

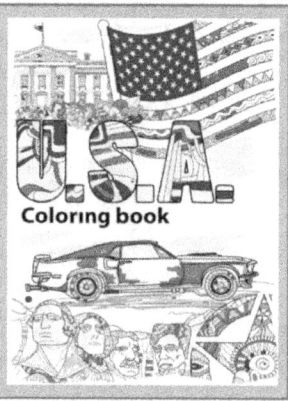

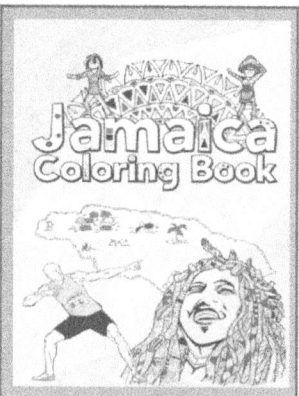

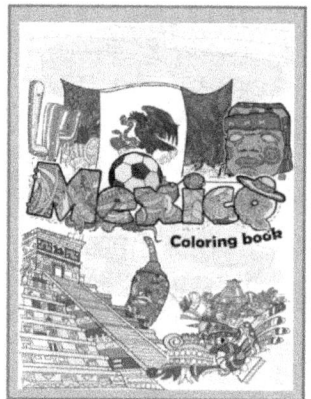

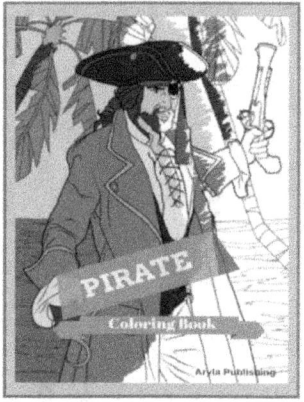

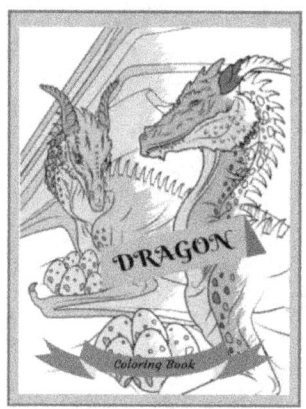

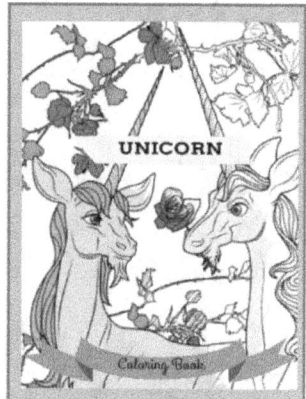

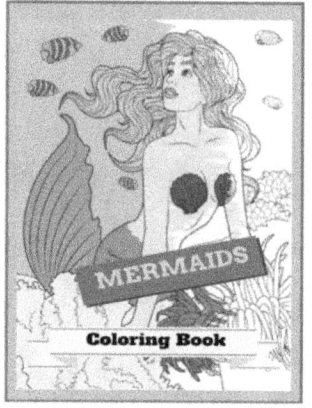

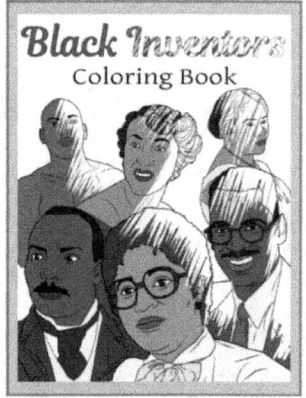

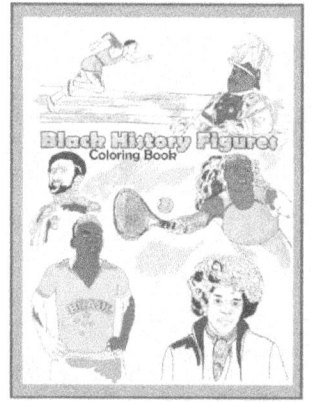

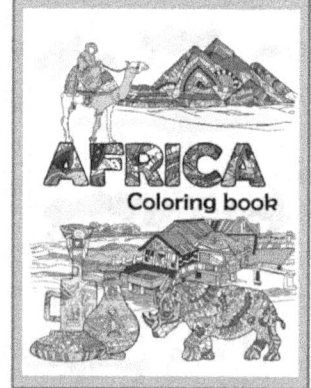

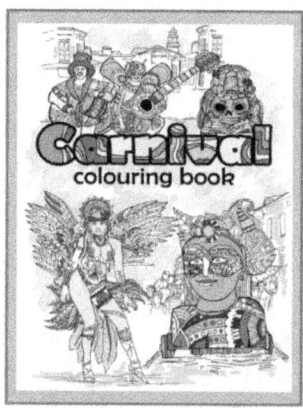

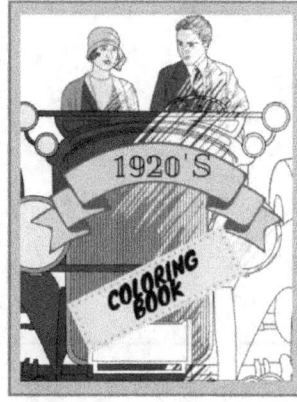

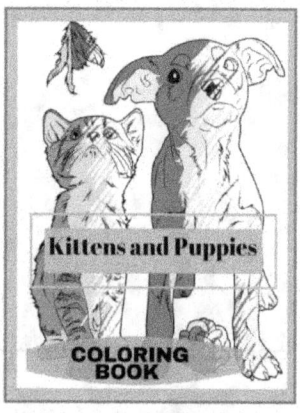

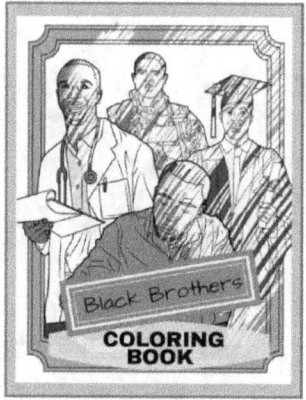

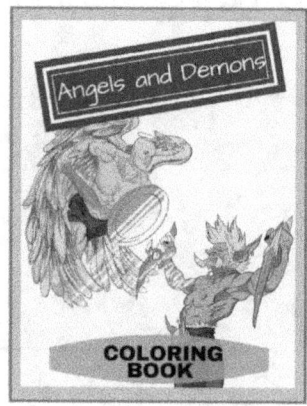

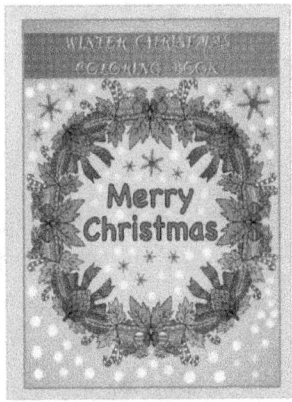
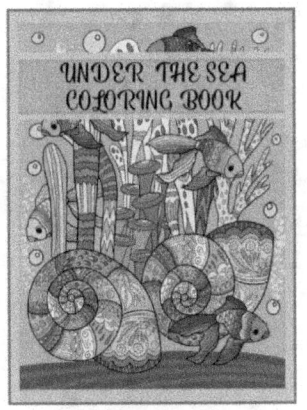
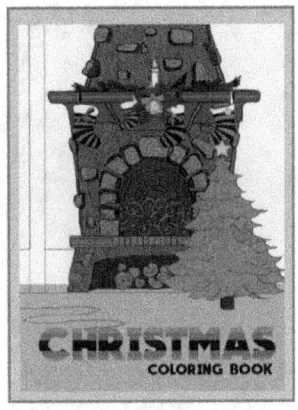
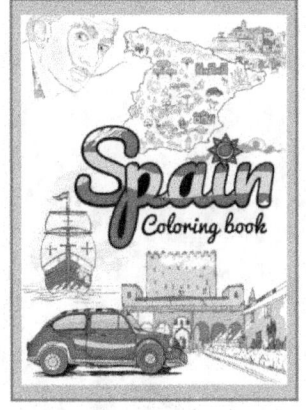
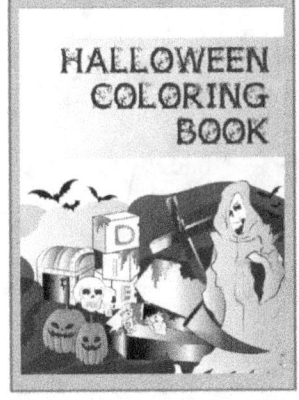
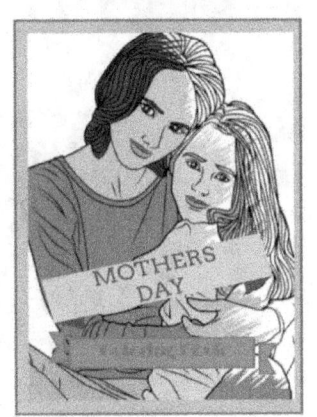
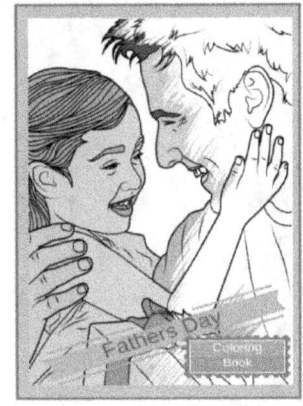

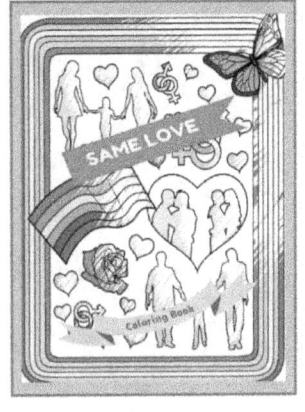
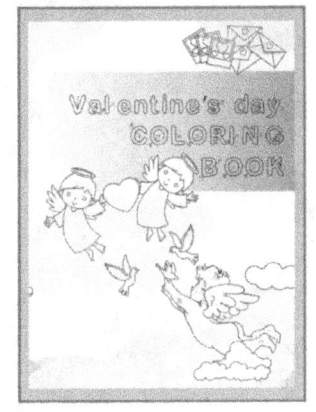
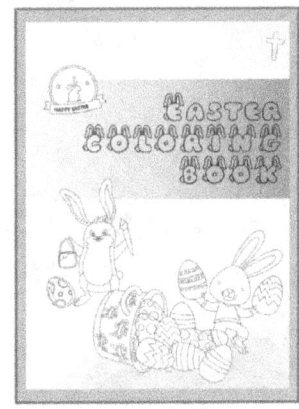
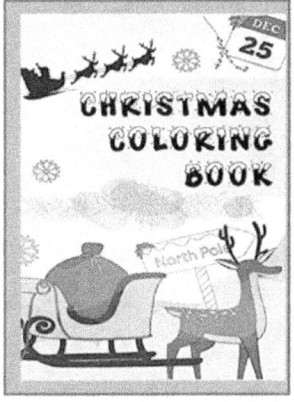
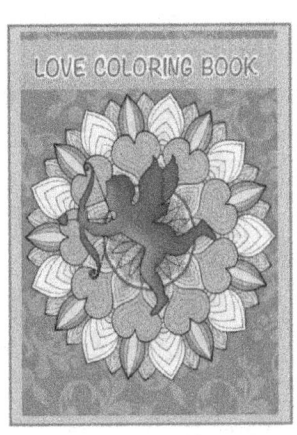
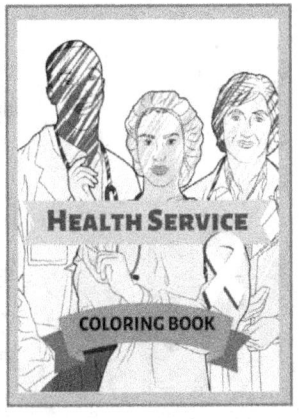
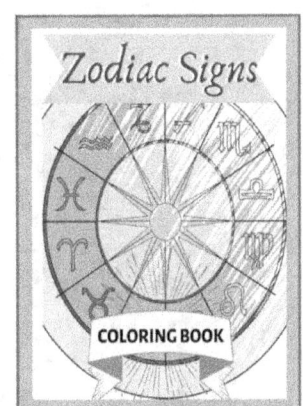
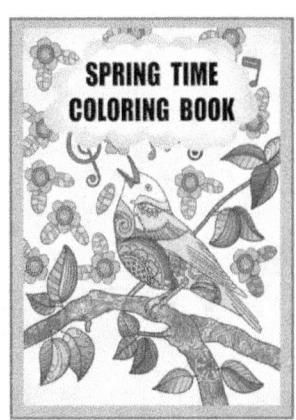

Color In Fun
Kids Books

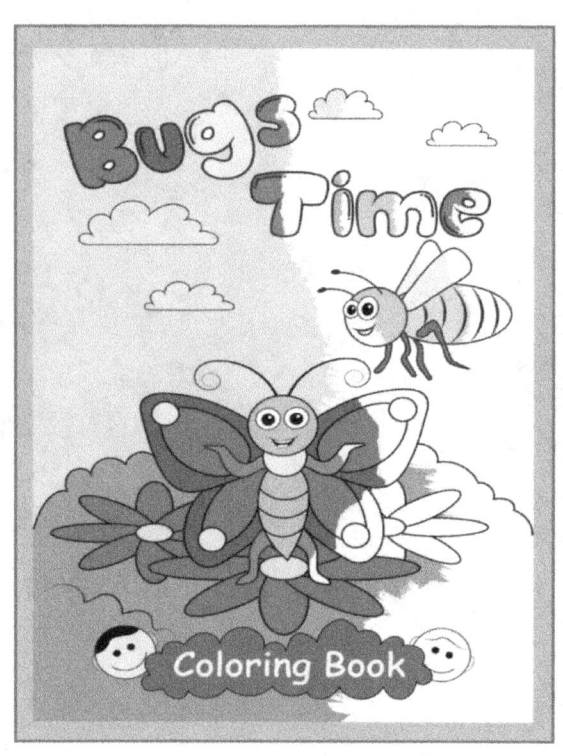

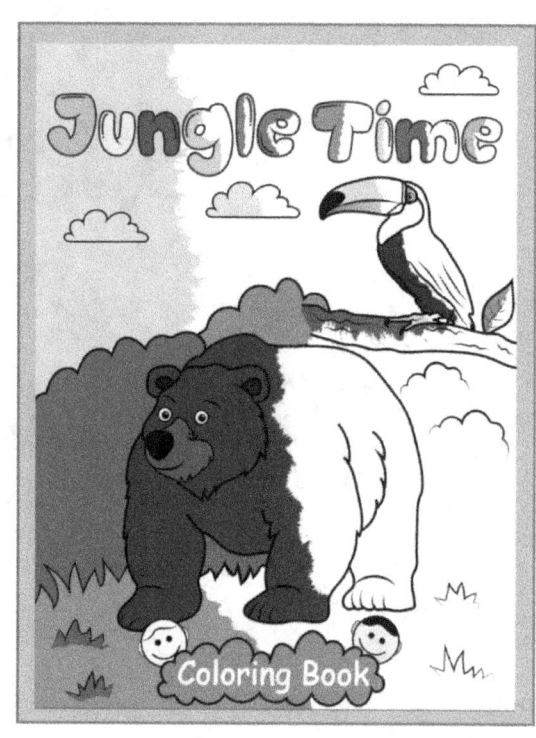

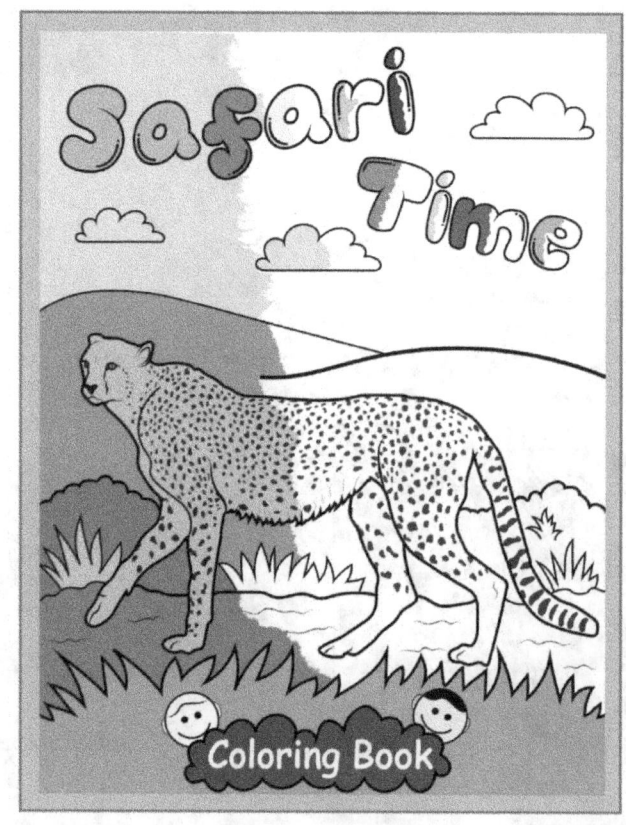

Visit **www.ArylaPublishing.com**
to find out about all new releases.

Follow us @arylapublishing on Twitter Instagram & Facebook

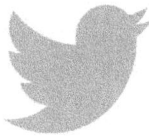  

Search for Aryla Publishing on

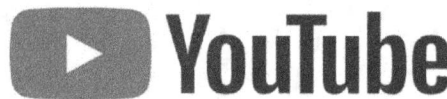 **YouTube**

Check out our <u>Book Trailers</u>

<u>Subscribe</u> **to keep up to date with new releases!**

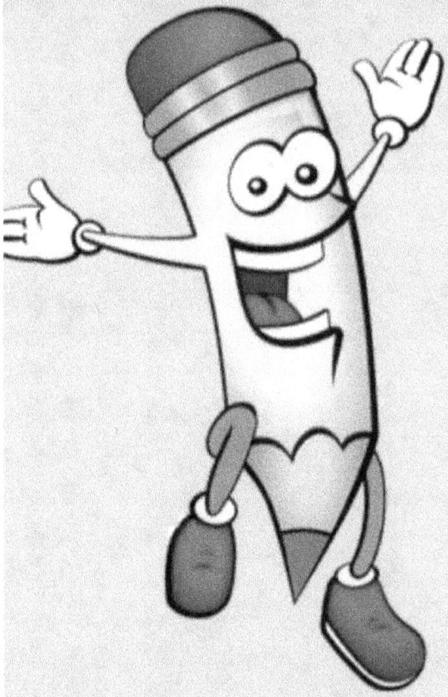

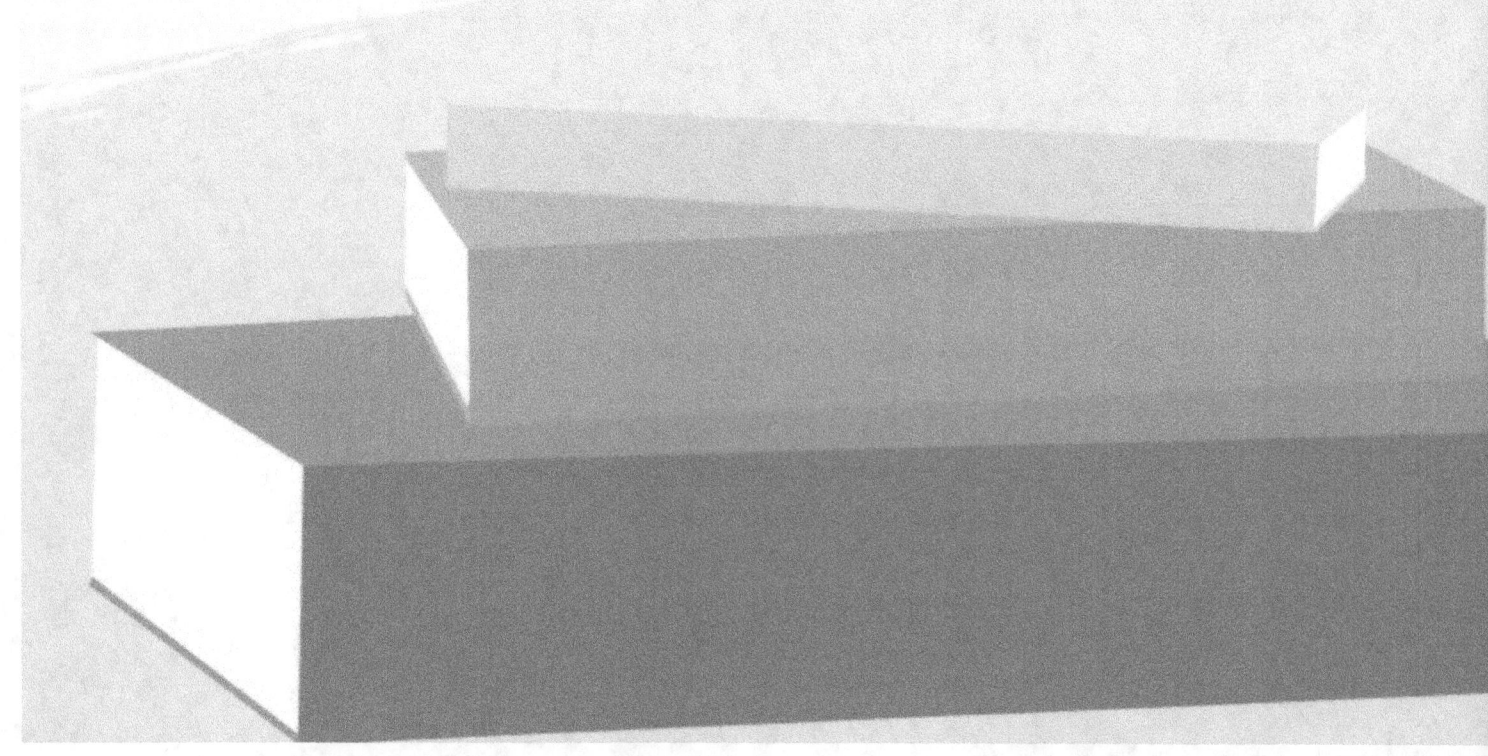

WE WOULD LOVE YOUR FEEDBACK

PLEASE LEAVE REVIEW AT:-

https://viewbook.at/Mothersdaycolor